LEADERS
WHO MAKE A
DIFFERENCE

LEADERSHIP LESSONS *from*
THREE GREAT BIBLE LEADERS

PAUL W.
CHAPPELL

First published in 2009 by Striving Together Publications, a
ministry of Lancaster Baptist Church, Lancaster, CA 93535. Striving
Together Publications is committed to providing tried, trusted,
and proven books that will further equip local churches to carry
out the Great Commission. Your comments and suggestions
are valued.

Striving Together Publications
4020 E. Lancaster Blvd.
Lancaster, CA 93535
800.201.7748
www.strivingtogether.com

Cover design by Andrew Jones
Layout by Craig Parker
Edited by Monica Bass and Tina Butterfield
Special thanks to our proofreaders.

ISBN 978-1-59894-083-1

Printed in the United States of America

Table of Contents

Introduction

When I was saved in 1972, my Sunday school teacher gave me a new Bible—an inexpensive, plastic-bound copy. I loved it and carried it everywhere I went! In the flyleaf of this Bible, I collected signatures and life verses from preachers who passed through our church and, in many cases, my home. I have the signatures of Dr. John R. Rice, Dr. B.R. Laken, Dr. G.B. Vick, Dr. Jerry Falwell, Dr. Jack Hyles, Dr. Monroe Parker, Dr. Myron Cedarholm, and many others.

I keep this Bible in my office, and reading these signatures stirs a deep gratitude for the heritage of godly leaders who invested in my early Christian life. I am privileged to have known and learned from men who walked with God, men whom God has used to make a difference in their generation.

Times have changed since 1972. Many of our leaders are in Heaven; some have fallen; and others have forsaken their positions. We desperately need godly leaders in this generation. We stand at a crossroads—spiritually and nationally—and our direction largely depends on our leaders.

The spiritual and moral decay of our nation is advancing so rapidly that we cannot and we must not look the other way optimistically hoping the corruption will reverse itself. The government and media are increasingly turning from indifference toward Christianity to intolerance of our God and His truths.

More grievous than repression from the government or the world is the compromise among our own. Pastors and other spiritual leaders are willing to negotiate and make concessions with the world to avoid the labels "divisive," "bigoted," or "intolerant." Laypeople are too timid to speak up for Christ, preferring to blend in with the world. Few are willing to be different enough to make a difference.

Will biblical Christianity become extinct in our generation? Is the glory so faded that it can never be reclaimed? Is the picture too marred to even consider saving the canvas?

Absolutely not! God often transforms the reprehensible into the beautiful, making it a worthy display of His glory. Great need is the easel on which God exhibits His greatest manifestations of power.

Consider the Israelites as they faced the land of Canaan. After forty years of wandering in the wilderness, they were finally standing before the very land God had promised to them. But their leader, Moses, had just died, and the land was already occupied by strong nations. The picture was one of overwhelming odds—until God raised up Joshua, and through him the land was conquered.

Consider Jerusalem after the city had lain desolate during Israel's captivity in Babylon. The Israelites had neither the money nor the motivation to rebuild the city, and the few who lived there were easy prey to the maltreatment of surrounding hostile nations. The picture was one of hopelessness—until God raised up Nehemiah, and through him the walls of the city were rebuilt.

Consider Jacob and his family during Palestine's famine, one so severe that they would have surely died of starvation without God's divine intervention. The picture was one of desperation—until God raised up Joseph, and through him the young nation of Israel was sustained and nourished.

Notice that in each of these situations, God did not begin His incredible demonstrations of power by changing the circumstances or conforming the masses. He began by raising up godly leaders.

What kind of leader does God choose? These pages examine the traits of these men whom God used to make a difference. These men were not born as world-shakers.

They were not wealthy or famous. They were simple men willing to be used by God to make a difference.

I believe that our greatest need today is not political change or moral reform but leaders who make a difference. We must have leaders who set the direction rather than follow the crowd. We need leaders who will, like Elisha, pick up the mantle of their predecessors and cry out, *"Where is the LORD God of Elijah?"* (2 Kings 2:14).

The men examined in these pages knew and served the same God we do. What God did for them, He will do for us. My prayer is that God would use this book to renew the ranks of leaders who make a difference.

PART ONE

Joshua

A LEADER WHO HAD VISION

To lead others, you must first know where you are going. Vision is essential to success, but too often Christian leadership is attempted without it. Personality, wealth, fame, and popularity can all attract a following, but none of these can replace a clear, God-given vision.

A biblical vision is essential for godly leadership. Proverbs 29:18 explains, *"Where there is no vision, the people perish...."* Biblical vision is seeing your area of oversight through the lens of God's Word.

Leaders who make a difference have a large vision. They know how to dream big, and they know how to share their dreams with others. Joshua was such a leader, and his vision came from God Himself.

"Every place that the sole of your foot shall tread upon, that have I given unto you, as I said unto Moses. From the wilderness and this Lebanon even unto the great river, the river Euphrates, all the land of the Hittites, and unto the great sea toward the going down of the sun, shall be your coast."
—JOSHUA 1:3–4

CHAPTER ONE

Vision Is Developed through Preparation

When we comprehend the dearth of godly leadership, our most natural response is to search for the shortest, fastest route to world-wide impact! After all, there's no time like the present. Shoddy preparation, however, will produce shoddy leadership.

We demand thorough preparation from those we allow to have lasting impact in our lives. We expect the lawyers we hire to have spent years in law school and significant time and energy preparing for our cases. We insist that our soldiers receive skill training and execute regular combat drills before they are thrust into war zones. We enroll our children in schools where we believe the teachers have diligently prepared for the classes they teach.

We believe in preparation for everyone else, but when it is our turn for preparation, we chafe at it. We try to wish it away or attempt a short-cut.

God takes no less pain to prepare His leaders than a coach his athletes, or a government its ambassadors. God uses times of preparation to equip us for His service. He uses these seasons to develop, clarify, and purify our vision.

Preparation cannot be successfully accomplished overnight; it is a process. How did this process unfold in Joshua's life?

Joshua Was Proven in Battle

"Then came Amalek, and fought with Israel in Rephidim. And Moses said unto Joshua, Choose us out men, and go out, fight with Amalek: to morrow I will stand on the top of the hill with the rod of God in mine hand."
—EXODUS 17:8–9

Before God appointed Joshua as the general and leader of Israel, He tested him in a wilderness battle. Moses assigned Joshua the tremendous responsibility of choosing the warriors and leading the battle against Amalek. But while Joshua fought, Moses interceded.

Joshua's later ministry description would require intense military leadership. During the battles for the conquest of the Promised Land, Joshua would not have

Moses standing on the hill interceding for him. He would bear the entire responsibility of the army and the battle. God used this battle with Amalek to prove Joshua and to develop his leadership potential.

As with Joshua, God sends custom designed proving grounds into each of our lives. To us, they look like inconveniences, added responsibilities, delays and obstacles to our plans, or painful situations. We tend either to balk at them because they are difficult or to feel frustrated by them because we want to move past them to reach our larger goals.

While we usually cannot see how these situations are going to be productive or helpful, God, who sees His purposes for our future, can. He sends them as opportunities to prove and develop us. Even Moses was first proven through forty years of shepherding before he was commissioned to lead Israel through the wilderness.

Joshua could not have been trusted to receive God's vision for his leadership had he not proven loyal under command. He could not have been relied upon as a combat general had he not proven faithful as a combat soldier.

There is no preparation for ministry like finding a place to serve in the battle and staying in it! Don't wait until the "big opportunity" comes your way; simply look for an opportunity to serve where you are.

God does not entrust men and women with leadership before He has proven them. Jesus stated: *"He that is faithful in that which is least is faithful also in* much: and he that is unjust in the least is unjust also in much" (Luke 16:10).

For God to entrust one with spiritual leadership before he has been proven, would endanger those under the leader's care. Paul specifically cautioned Timothy against assigning leadership in the local church to those who have not been proven.

"And let these also first be proved; then let them use the office of a deacon, being found blameless."
—1 TIMOTHY 3:10

"Lay hands suddenly on no man, neither be partaker of other men's sins: keep thyself pure."—1 TIMOTHY 5:22

Embrace the seasons of proving God gives you— develop through the difficulties, and mature through the monotony.

Joshua Was Prepared through Serving

"And Moses rose up, and his minister Joshua: and Moses went up into the mount of God."—EXODUS 24:13

The word *minister* in this verse means "servant." Joshua, a man who would later lead the conquest of the Promised Land, did not think it beneath him to be the servant, the burden bearer, of Moses. The measure of a man's greatness is not how many people serve him but how many he serves. Jesus told His disciples that the greatest of all is the servant of all (Matthew 23:11–12).

You are not a lesser man because you serve your wife and your children, seek for opportunities to help others at work, and find ways to better your community. You are not a lesser woman because you give of yourself to your church, invest in your children, and make serving your husband your highest priority next to honoring the Lord.

Young people especially need to learn to serve. When they give to those who can offer them nothing in return, they develop an understanding of what leadership is all about—servanthood. Winning souls, visiting in rest homes, taking missions trips, delivering pies to widows—all of these are avenues to developing a servant's heart.

Jesus Himself *"came not to be ministered unto, but to minister…"* (Mark 10:45). In our flesh we love to be "ministered unto"—especially we who are in leadership. We expect others to offer the perks due us because of our positions, but this attitude does not reflect the heart of Christ.

"Let this mind be in you, which was also in Christ Jesus: Who, being in the form of God, thought it not robbery to be equal with God: But made himself of no reputation, and took upon him the form of a servant, and was made in the likeness of men: And being found in fashion as a man, he humbled himself, and became obedient unto death, even the death of the cross."—PHILIPPIANS 2:5–8

Christ emptied Himself of His prerogatives to rule and command, to be served and honored. In that emptying, He did not cease being God. He just laid aside His rights and willingly became the servant. The heart of a servant is the heart of Christ.

But when we are confronted with need, our most natural response is to compare our "job description" with the need. If it doesn't fit, we dismiss the need with the cliché, "That's not my job."

Jesus taught, however, that one with a servant's heart goes beyond the call of duty: "*So likewise ye, when ye shall have done all those things which are commanded you, say, We are unprofitable servants: we have done that which was our duty to do*" (Luke 17:10).

The man or woman with a true servant's heart views every need he can meet as part of his job description. Joshua didn't serve Moses because he was required to but because he had a servant's heart.

Joshua Was Patient in Waiting

"And Moses went into the midst of the cloud, and gat him up into the mount: and Moses was in the mount forty days and forty nights."—Exodus 24:18

For most of us, forty days of waiting is forty days too long! But while Moses was receiving the Ten Commandments on Mount Sinai, Joshua's task was to wait.

Patience is not my greatest strength! I remember some years ago, as we were preparing to go to Colorado for vacation, I told my wife, "Honey, tomorrow morning we are going to start our vacation early. If we get up at four, we can be on the road by six. That way we can get through the desert before it gets too hot." My wife, the godly, submissive wife she is, said, "All right, sweetheart, we'll be glad to do that."

Sunday had been a busy day at church, and we returned home late that night. Monday morning I was sleeping very soundly when four o'clock came…and went. When I woke up around seven, I bolted out of bed and began rousing everyone else. We all grabbed the suitcases and threw them into the car. We were finally on our way!

As we drove through the desert, I asked for my sunglasses. My wife said they were in our blue suitcase, so I asked my son Larry to get them. After searching the back of the car, he informed me that there was no blue suitcase. I asked my wife which blue suitcase, and she responded, "The one I told you to get from the top of the stairs as we were rushing out of the house." We stopped in Flagstaff, Arizona, to buy new sunglasses and replacements for some of the other contents of that suitcase. What a waste of time and money!

I learned that day that my impatience had cost me. In my life and in the lives of others, I have seen spiritual blessings lost because of impatience.

Waiting while God is enlarging your vision is difficult, and in our rush to get things done, we easily get ahead of God's timing; we also rush ahead of God's blessings. Some preparation can be accomplished only through waiting.

Besides being tempted with impatience, Joshua could have been tempted with jealousy. While Moses was enjoying the privilege of communing intimately with God in a way no other man had (Numbers 12:6–8), Joshua was asked to wait below. If Joshua had been like many of us, he would have spent those forty days frustrated that he wasn't invited as well. After all, being Moses' servant should surely entitle him to benefits!

Jealousy is a subtle but deadly enemy of vision. It constricts one's vision, turning his focus from what he desires to do for God's glory to what he feels he has missed unjustly. Jealousy also ravages the leader who becomes infected with it. I have seen jealousy ruin more leaders than even immorality. Scripture provides many examples of jealousy's damaging effects on leaders.

Consider how jealousy transformed Saul (1 Samuel 18:8–9) from a humble king to an insanely angry and vengeful man-hunter.

Consider how jealousy prompted Joseph's brothers (Acts 7:9), Israel's patriarchs, to sell their own brother into slavery.

Consider how jealousy corrupted the Hebrew chief priests (Mark 15:10–14), causing them to crucify their Messiah, rather than receive Him.

Jealousy can cause irreparable damage.

"A sound heart is the life of the flesh: but envy the rottenness of the bones."—PROVERBS 14:30

"Wrath is cruel, and anger is outrageous; but who is able to stand before envy?"—PROVERBS 27:4

True servants don't have envious hearts. Even during Joshua's time of waiting, he kept a servant's heart. He didn't spend those forty days stewing over missed opportunity or position. As Moses descended from the mount, he found Joshua right where he had left him, still ready to serve (Exodus 32:17).

Joshua didn't greet Moses with the bitter cry, "Why not me?" because Joshua wasn't aspiring to leadership. He was content to serve, and God used his patience to transform him into a godly leader.

The best thing a leader can do is to wait on the Lord. This principle is especially imperative concerning making major life decisions during a time of loss or grief. I've seen many Christians who, under pressure, made decisions that led them away from God's will and God's work.

Before you resign your Sunday school class or bus route, leave your church, decide to move, or make other decisions with long-range consequences, seek wise, godly counsel. Sometimes decisions such as these are made simply because one is frustrated with waiting.

We often rush ahead of God rather than wait on His timing. In our rush to get things done, we get ahead of God and miss out on His blessings. Rather than becoming impatient, we must place the situation in God's hands and give Him full control of the timing and the outcome.

Preparation for leadership always involves waiting. God is not wasting your time when He gives you the task of waiting; He is preparing you for greater vision.

"Wait on the Lord: be of good courage, and he shall strengthen thine heart: wait, I say, on the LORD."—PSALM 27:14

Joshua Was Pure in His Vision

"Blessed are the pure in heart: for they shall see God."
—MATTHEW 5:8

When the heart is pure, the vision is clear. Joshua was not a self-promoter or an egomaniac; he saw things clearly as they pertained to the will of God. Numbers 13 gives us an example of his pure-hearted vision.

"And the LORD spake unto Moses, saying, Send thou men, that they may search the land of Canaan, which I give unto the children of Israel: of every tribe of their fathers shall ye send a man, every one a ruler among them. And Moses by the commandment of the LORD sent them from the wilderness of Paran: all those men were heads of the children of Israel."
—NUMBERS 13:1–3

The spies, sent to search out the Promised Land, could be likened to a Baptist committee. Instead of looking to God's promises, they fed on one another's perception of the impossibility before them—conquering the land God had promised.

God's great works have not come through committees but through leaders who were totally surrendered to Him. While ten of the twelve committee members were fearful of the giants and battle, Joshua fixed his focus on God. He had the pure vision to focus on God's clearly revealed will rather than on the obstacles to fulfilling it.

"And Joshua the son of Nun, and Caleb the son of Jephunneh, which were of them that searched the land, rent their clothes: And they spake unto all the company of the children of Israel, saying, The land, which we passed through to search it, is an exceeding good land. If the LORD delight in us, then he will bring us into this land, and give it us; a land which floweth with milk and honey. Only rebel not ye against the LORD, neither fear ye the people of the land; for they are bread for us: their defence is departed from them, and the LORD is with us: fear them not. But all the congregation bade stone them with stones. And the glory of the LORD appeared in the tabernacle of the congregation before all the children of Israel."—NUMBERS 14:6–10

A pattern oft repeated in the lives of leaders who make a difference is the opposition that comes as they edge closer to being used of God. It's as if the devil senses the potential for God's power to flow through their surrendered lives and plants doubts in their minds and accusations in the minds of others. "You're not good enough," "You can't do it," "You'll never see people saved," "It can't be done," "No one wants to hear what you have to say"—these thoughts are common darts of discouragement the devil hurls at leaders.

The person who places confidence in personal ability, education, friendships, allegiances, or alliances, will fail indeed. But while there will always be the naysayers who insist that God's will cannot be done, a Spirit-filled leader will place his confidence solely in God Almighty and press forward.

Joshua knew the victory would not come through his sword, his ingenuity, or his military skill. But he also knew that if God was in it, God would do it. This knowledge gave him the confidence to insist, against the voice of his peers, *"If the Lord delight in us, then he will bring us into this land, and give it us"* (Numbers 14:8).

In a world of ideals, such leadership would be appreciated and readily followed. But the results in Joshua's life were not quite so rosy. For believing God and trying to lead others to do the same, Joshua became a target. The people wanted to take the life of this faith-filled man of God!

If you will be a spiritual leader where you work—a man of God who doesn't laugh at improper jokes or join in ungodly conversation—if you will be distinct and stand for what is right, not everyone will applaud. You may be mocked, criticized, and ostracized. Standing for Christ may be difficult at times, but it does make a difference.

Like Joshua, we must understand the importance of vision and be willing to make sacrifices to lead others. For *"where there is no vision, the people perish..."* (Proverbs 29:18).

In 1986, when my family and I arrived in Lancaster to pastor Lancaster Baptist Church, the church was running an average attendance of twenty each week. When I had a Gospel tract printed to give out in the community, I described, not what the church was, but what it was going to be.

On one side of the tract, I described our church: "Independent, fundamental, Bible-believing, Baptist church." On the other side, I presented the programs available in our church: "exciting Sunday school, vibrant music, active youth ministry." Frankly, our Sunday school and music and youth ministries were nearly nonexistent at that time. But looking over the past twenty-four years, I'm amazed at how God has blessed these visionary phrases.

God, through His Word, had placed a vision in my heart for what He wanted our church to become, and I didn't want to settle for less. God will place a vision in your heart for your children, your ministry, your responsibilities. Dream this vision, and work to implement it. Joshua held a vision in his heart that God's people would possess the Promised Land, and this vision propelled him to lead.

But remember, Joshua was proven through service before he was commissioned as the leader. He learned to wait on God's timing, and during this time of waiting, his vision was sharpened. This is the pattern God uses in preparing leaders—preparation before responsibility.

Preparation never takes place overnight; it is a process. Though it may seem frustrating at times, submit to God's process of preparation in your life. Invest your life in serving others, and let God sharpen and purify your vision during the wait.

Joshua's life is a testimony to all of us that the vision God develops through a season of preparation is worth the investment!

CHAPTER TWO

Vision Is Mobilized through a Plan

If every good and biblical vision that has ever been conceived in the hearts of godly people were achieved, our world would be reached for Christ! Unfortunately, visions themselves do not guarantee success. Without a clear plan, a vision will stagnate or dissipate.

A vision will motivate, but a plan will mobilize.

When God placed Joshua in a leadership position, Joshua didn't simply dream about success; he put feet to his dreams.

> *"Then Joshua commanded the officers of the people, saying, Pass through the host, and command the people, saying, Prepare you victuals; for within three days ye shall pass over this Jordan, to go in to possess the land, which the LORD your God giveth you to possess it."*—JOSHUA 1:10–11

When Joshua led Israel to enter the Promised Land, the land was still full of giants and enemy nations. Joshua didn't yet know that Jesus, the Captain of the Lord of Hosts, would meet him outside the city of Jericho. He didn't know that God was going to destroy the walls of Jericho just by the Israelites' marching around them. He didn't know that in some battles the enemy would simply turn and flee. Even without knowing all the miracles God would do to give the Israelites the Promised Land, Joshua refused to question the orders of an Almighty God.

Parents, particularly fathers, are called to lead their children. In many homes, however, the children lead the parents! As parents, you should listen to your children and strive to meet their needs, but don't let them dictate the direction of your home.

A pastor is called to shepherd his church. He is to direct the church to fulfill the Great Commission. Rather than view this command as an insurmountable task, he must mobilize his people with a plan to accomplish God's directions.

Every leader needs a vision from God of the direction his followers need to go, and then he needs to lead. Use your position of leadership to influence those you lead to take clear steps of biblical action.

Joshua's leadership responsibility included leading the people to a specific location—the Promised Land. Accomplishing this task required that he focus his eyes clearly on the goal. The people may have been content to linger in the wilderness, but Joshua knew where they were heading, and he pushed them to move forward.

We can easily stagnate in our spiritual growth. We become satisfied and complacent with our past victories and present comforts. God uses the spiritual leaders in our lives to help us and nudge us to higher ground.

A plan helps to remind us that, just as for the Israelites, our goal is not just survival; it is advancement.

"Every place that the sole of your foot shall tread upon, that have I given unto you, as I said unto Moses. From the wilderness and this Lebanon even unto the great river, the river Euphrates, all the land of the Hittites, and unto the great sea toward the going down of the sun, shall be your coast."
—Joshua 1:3–4

What is your goal for your children? Your Sunday school class? Your area of responsibility? If your goal is simply maintaining a current status (survival), you cannot fulfill God's calling as a leader.

Your primary goal should be that your family, your ministry, your life, and your career glorify God. Ask God to give you a specific vision of how you can best lead your followers to glorify God. Know where you are going, and claim God's promises to get there.

God had promised the Israelites a vast amount of land, but they never claimed more than ten percent of it. This tendency is typical of most Christians today.

I believe there are men who, because of a lack of faith or prayer, never got to see God bless their business with success.

I believe there are families who never got to see God work through their family for His glory because they were comfortable simply to maintain.

I believe there are churches all over America that have never come close to reaching their potential. Christ gave us the command to evangelize the entire world, and with the command, the power to do it. *"But ye shall receive power, after that the Holy Ghost is come upon you: and ye shall be witnesses unto me both in Jerusalem, and in all Judaea, and in Samaria, and unto the uttermost part of the earth"* (Acts 1:8).

Because we do not have clearly laid plans, we easily lose our vision and give up our communities to the cults of our day. Each church must accomplish worldwide evangelization through strategic planning, including church planting (here in America and worldwide) and saturating their immediate area with the Gospel.

What an exciting privilege and responsibility to claim land for Christ! It will take leaders who make a difference through systematic planning to see this opportunity realized.

Motivating others with a plan involves understanding the principle of ownership. God has entrusted you with a sphere of responsibility—claim that for the Lord.

Andrew, a young boy in our church, was at home one day when he noticed two Jehovah's Witnesses coming down his street. He jumped up and called out, "Mom, quick, I need some tracts. Some Jehovah's Witnesses are coming, and I'm going to head them off!" He grabbed a handful of tracts and hurried to each house to invite his neighbors to our church. He positioned himself so that he would run into the Jehovah's Witnesses within a few doors.

When he met them, he informed them, "I'm from Lancaster Baptist Church, and I already have this street taken care of." They weren't quite sure what to do, so they crossed to the other side of the street. Andrew ran to the other side of the street and repeated his previous plan. Again he met the Jehovah's Witnesses, and again he informed them, "I've got this street covered." His plan worked; they returned to their car and left.

Godly leaders are good stewards of the vision God has given them, and they develop a plan to claim their territory for the Lord. Expand and broaden your vision so you can fulfill all God would have you do.

A young pastor arrived at his new church enthusiastic about what he knew God wanted to accomplish through him. He placed on his desk a plaque which read, "Win the world for Christ."

His church members felt uncomfortable with this big vision. They had been content to maintain the status quo and feared being pulled out of their comfort zone, so they immediately questioned his sign. "How can you reach the world for Christ?" they asked. Some accused him of being on an ego trip. Others discouraged him saying, "It just can't be done using Bible methods."

The more the pastor thought about the difficulty of reaching the world for Christ, the more impossible it seemed, and the more discouraged he became. Soon, he replaced his sign. The new one read, "Win some for Christ."

In the next few months, more problems arose in the church, and it seemed no one cared to support this pastor in his efforts to reach others with the Gospel. Every day when he looked at his sign, instead of becoming motivated by it, he became discouraged. He wasn't reaching new people; he was struggling to keep the people he had.

Once again, the pastor changed his sign. It now reads, "Try not to lose too many."

While I don't know of any pastor who would literally place such a sign on his desk, I'm afraid that too many of us have a similar sign in our minds. We must not allow our vision to be narrowed or our goal lowered to minimal survival.

Dream big, and plan thoroughly. Have a goal so big that it will only be reached through God's power, but remember that God empowers those who are moving. Clearly define your goal through the lens of Scripture, and take definite steps of action to reach it. Like Joshua, mobilize the vision God has developed in your heart through a definite plan of action.

CHAPTER THREE

Vision Is Realized through Provision

If we have the magnitude of vision God desires for us to have, we will quickly find that we do not have the ability to see this vision realized in our own flesh. God-given vision can be accomplished only through God-given provision.

We sometimes mistakenly perceive our greatest need in reaching our spiritual goals to be money. Indeed, money is needed; we need gas to go soulwinning, supplies to construct buildings, etc. Money is a necessary part of ministry and has been since Old Testament days when the tabernacle was constructed. But money is not the main ingredient needed.

God Provides His Presence

The most crucial of God's provisions to Joshua is our paramount need as well: God's own presence.

"There shall not any man be able to stand before thee all the days of thy life: as I was with Moses, so I will be with thee: I will not fail thee, nor forsake thee."—JOSHUA 1:5

The God who was with Moses as he stood before Pharaoh to relay God's demand, "Let My people go!" was also with Joshua. The God who parted the Red Sea, provided water from a rock, and sent bread from Heaven for Moses was with Joshua. In God, Joshua had all he needed.

God's presence was not available just to yesteryear's heroes of the faith; it is promised to every child of God. We serve a God whose presence is with us every step of the way. He promised us, *"I will never leave thee, nor forsake thee"* (Hebrews 13:5).

A truly God-given vision cannot be accomplished through self-effort. Fortunately, we have no need to rely on self-effort, for God has promised us His power: *"Not by might, nor by power, but by my spirit, saith the LORD of hosts"* (Zechariah 4:6).

Those leaders we look to as great heroes of the past were simply men and women who were surrendered to and led by the Holy Spirit.

Years ago a group of preachers were discussing who they should invite to preach for a revival meeting they were planning. An older pastor in the group suggested the famous evangelist, D.L. Moody. A younger pastor, with a tinge of jealousy countered, "Why do we have to have D.L. Moody? Does he have a monopoly on the Holy Spirit?"

"No," the older pastor replied, "but the Holy Spirit has a monopoly on him."

This story illustrates the requirement for accessing God's power—yielding to the Holy Spirit. The Holy Spirit indwells every child of God, and He is available to lead, guide, and empower you as you lead others to realize God's vision.

In the same breath that Christ gave the Great Commission (a task far too big for us to accomplish in our own might), He promised His presence.

"Go ye therefore, and teach all nations, baptizing them in the name of the Father, and of the Son, and of the Holy Ghost: Teaching them to observe all things whatsoever I have commanded you: and, lo, I am with you alway, even unto the end of the world. Amen."—Matthew 28:19–20

G. Campbell Morgan was preaching in a rest home on this text. After reading the words, "Lo, I am with you alway, even unto the end of the world," he paused to comment. "Isn't that a wonderful promise?"

One lady spoke up quickly. "That is not a wonderful promise," she contradicted.

Dr. Morgan looked at her in surprise. "It's not a wonderful promise," she explained. "It's a wonderful reality." This dear lady understood not only that God had promised to be with her always, but that He was present at that very moment.

It's a pivotal point in your life and leadership when these guarantees of God's presence aren't just promises to store away, but they are the reality of your daily life. God's presence is God's greatest provision for any need you face.

God Provides His Word

In addition to His presence, God gave Joshua another great provision—His Word. What a treasure! This was a treasure God commanded Joshua not to waste through neglect but to meditate on day and night. *"This book of the law shall not depart out of thy mouth; but thou shalt meditate therein day and night, that thou mayest observe to do according to all that is written therein: for then thou shalt make thy way prosperous, and then thou shalt have good success"* (Joshua 1:8).

When God gave Joshua the responsibility to assume Moses' role as Israel's leader, He expected Joshua to lead the people with God's Word. God wanted His law to flow out of Joshua's mouth as naturally as any other speech. He wanted Joshua's first response to every situation to be biblical. He wanted Joshua's advice to be scriptural. God wanted Joshua's entire focus to be centered on Him.

What did God promise Joshua in return for this dedicated concentration on His Word? Success. God has promised to honor those who honor Him (1 Samuel 2:30).

Sometimes, Christian businessmen tell me they've decided to miss their church's midweek Bible study to get ahead in their businesses. But they have a mistaken idea of what will bring true success. The only time the word "success" is used in Scripture is in Joshua 1:8. Here,

God promises success to those who are meditating on and living out the Word of God.

If you need to chop down a large tree with an ax, choosing to sharpen the ax first will not waste your time; it will multiply the fruit of your efforts. Likewise, time spent in Bible study is not a waste; it is opening your life to receive God's prospering success.

Jesus taught that God's Word has been specially preserved for all ages: "*For verily I say unto you, Till heaven and earth pass, one jot or one tittle shall in no wise pass from the law, till all be fulfilled*" (Matthew 5:18).

The psalmist, too, recorded the value of God's preserved Word: "*The words of the LORD are pure words: as silver tried in a furnace of earth, purified seven times. Thou shalt keep them, O LORD, thou shalt preserve them from this generation for ever*" (Psalm 12:6–7).

When we meditate on the perfectly preserved Word of God, it becomes part of us, and we apply it to every situation we face. We procure its wisdom to counsel those we serve. It gives direction to lead others.

Some people mark their Bibles, but spiritual leaders allow the Bible to mark them. They don't just study the Bible; they obey it. And they teach its truths to those they lead.

These two great resources—God's presence and God's Word—work together. God's Word promises us God's presence, and God's presence guides us in our application of God's Word.

Our greatest visions are nothing without the avail of God's power. To be a leader who understands God's vision for you and your ministry, be a leader who walks with God. Depend on God's presence, and faithfully meditate on His Word.

God still desires to make a difference using leaders who have vision. If you, like Joshua, are willing to receive God's vision through preparation, to mobilize the vision with a biblical plan, and to accomplish the vision with God's provision, then only God knows what He can and will do through your life!

Joshua's life proves that God is *"able to do exceeding abundantly above all that we ask or think, according to the power that worketh in us"* (Ephesians 3:20).

PART TWO

Nehemiah

A LEADER WHO BROUGHT REVIVAL

One of the most devastating days in Jewish history took place around 586 BC when the Babylonians invaded Jerusalem for the third and final time. Nebuchadnezzar destroyed the city: he burned the walls and ransacked the temple.

About seventy years later, a faithful remnant was allowed to return to Jerusalem to rebuild the temple. For the first time in many years there was hope for revival in Israel—the nation's return to the worship of their true God.

With the walls of Jerusalem still decimated, however, those in the city were in constant peril. The enemies of Israel could easily access the city to persecute those who had a heart to worship God. Of a greater concern, they could influence the Israelites to pervert their worship.

When Nehemiah, a Hebrew captive in Babylon, heard about the plight of Jerusalem, he prayerfully planned to make a difference. However, as soon as the Jew's enemies discovered Nehemiah's intention to rebuild the walls, they mounted opposition. But Nehemiah was a leader—a man who could lead his people even in the face of impossibilities.

Our situation today is no less dire than that of Jerusalem in Nehemiah's day. Our world stands in desperate need of revival, and many say it can never happen. We need leaders who will follow Nehemiah's example and make a difference.

CHAPTER FOUR

Revival Is Initiated by Supplication

Nehemiah understood that revival cannot be drummed up by self-effort. His first response to Jerusalem's need was not a frenzy of activity—soliciting the sympathy of others or planning how to manipulate the king to send a construction crew to the city.

As one preacher observed, "Anything done in my own strength is bound to fail miserably or to succeed even more miserably." If the work depends on our skill, ingenuity, or resources, it will never be a great work.

We all acknowledge our dependence on God in word, yet how many times have we experienced situations of great need but given it little prayer?

Nehemiah's response to this tremendous need was prayer, and his prayer was the starting point for the rebuilding of the walls. Let's examine four aspects of

Nehemiah's prayer to learn how we can strengthen our prayers for revival.

Nehemiah's Prayer Began with a Burden

"And it came to pass, when I heard these words, that I sat down and wept, and mourned certain days, and fasted, and prayed before the God of heaven,"—NEHEMIAH 1:4

Burdens have a way of motivating us to pray. Many times God allows burdens to come into our lives simply to draw us closer to Him.

Hudson Taylor, missionary to China, aptly pointed out, "It does not matter how great the pressure is, only where the pressure lies. Do not allow the pressure to come between you and the Lord. Then no matter how great the pressure, it only serves to press you closer to His heart."

We want to be used of God, but, for us, as for Nehemiah, being used will require assuming the weight of a burden. Sometimes this burden is the weight of a personal need, but it often should be the weight of others' needs.

God commands us to "bear…one another's burdens" (Galatians 6:2), but in our full schedules, we become too busy to see beyond our own needs.

A five-year-old boy was riding to McDonald's with his dad. On their way, they saw that two cars had collided in the middle of the road. As they approached the scene of the accident, the father suggested his son pray for the situation. "Dear God," the boy immediately began, "don't let this car block our way to McDonald's." Sadly, our prayers, when they do include others, are often just as selfish.

R.A. Torrey addressed this problem of being too busy to pray: "We are too busy to pray, and so we are too busy to have power. We have a great deal of activity, but we accomplish little; many services but few conversions; much machinery but few results."

Our prayers must move beyond the most basic, tangible needs to the spiritual issues at stake. When Nehemiah discovered the anguish of his hometown, he realized that the greatest crisis was that God's name was under attack. This burden motivated him to earnest prayer.

Nehemiah's prayer was no trite "bless all the people in Jerusalem." His weeping and mourning reveals the heart of a man who agonized before God over this spiritual burden. Broken-hearted leadership is less glamorous than wall-building leadership, but it must come first. Do you have a broken heart for your realm of responsibility? Do you care enough to pray?

Nehemiah's burden was further demonstrated by his fasting. Fasting is an outward evidence of our inner hunger to see God answer prayer. It is a self-denial that develops our prayer life. Fasting says to God, "More than food or any other pleasure, I desire Your power."

Jesus explained to His disciples that some prayers will only be brought to their fullest capacity through fasting. *"This kind can come forth by nothing, but by prayer and fasting"* (Mark 9:29).

Prayer and fasting are still the language God hears in this hour. Nehemiah's humble fasting revealed his hunger for God's intervention. His passion is a challenge to us all.

Nehemiah's Prayer Burned with Compassion

"Let thine ear now be attentive, and thine eyes open, that thou mayest hear the prayer of thy servant, which I pray before thee now, day and night, for the children of Israel thy servants…."
—NEHEMIAH 1:6

When Nehemiah heard about the needs of others, he felt *their* burden. He was not living in Jerusalem at that time. He did not personally need the protection of Jerusalem's walls. His burden was for others.

Our own needs weigh heavily on us because we are confronted with them every day; they alter our lives. Leaders who make a difference, however, feel other's needs as they do their own, and they passionately pray for the needs of those they serve.

In a speech at the 1996 Republican National Convention, Oklahoma representative J.C. Watts described compassion: "Compassion can't be measured in dollars and cents. It does come with a price tag, but the price tag isn't the amount of money spent, the price tag is love…."

Great leaders are not tough guys who force others to give them their way; great leaders are men and women who have hearts of compassion. This compassion makes a difference in others' lives.

We learn compassion from Jesus Himself. When Jesus saw people, He saw past their demanding needs, ungrateful and irreverent attitudes, and obnoxious idiosyncrasies because He saw through the eyes of compassion. *"But when he saw the multitudes, he was moved with compassion on them, because they fainted, and were scattered abroad, as sheep having no shepherd"* (Matthew 9:36).

Paul also cared deeply for the spiritual needs of the lost. Even during a "down time," while he waited in Athens for his ministry partners, *"his spirit was stirred in him, when he saw the city wholly given to idolatry"* (Acts 17:16). He felt compassion for the spiritual needs of people around him.

In the early years of our ministry in Lancaster, my wife Terrie and I would often spend our evenings together at a crest overlooking much of the valley in which we serve. We'd look across the valley at the many lights and pray for the people they represented.

I now have many special spots around the valley where I spend time in prayer. I ask God to touch hearts and soften them to the Gospel. I pray that souls would be saved, drunkards would be made sober, families would get back together—that God would do a mighty work.

Do you pray with compassion for the city where you live? Leaders who make a difference pray with burdened compassion because they know that only God can mend shattered lives, heal broken hearts, and satisfy spiritual hunger.

Nehemiah's Prayer Built on Confession

"…and confess the sins of the children of Israel, which we have sinned against thee: both I and my father's house have sinned. We have dealt very corruptly against thee, and have not kept the commandments, nor the statutes, nor the judgments, which thou commandedst thy servant Moses."
—NEHEMIAH 1:6–7

There are many in leadership today who have mastered the "blame game," and when these leaders get together, blame ricochets everywhere.

A spiritual leader, however, admits when he has done wrong. Nehemiah was transparent with God. He knew that the reason for Israel's captivity was their idolatry. Before he asked for timber to build the walls or for a work crew, he asked for forgiveness.

Daniel, another leader who made a difference through prayer for national restoration, also built his prayer on confession.

"And I set my face unto the Lord God, to seek by prayer and supplications, with fasting, and sackcloth, and ashes: And I prayed unto the LORD my God, and made my confession, and said, O Lord, the great and dreadful God, keeping the covenant and mercy to them that love him, and to them that keep his commandments; We have sinned, and have committed iniquity, and have done wickedly, and have rebelled, even by departing from thy precepts and from thy judgments: Neither have we hearkened unto thy servants the prophets, which spake in thy name to our kings, our princes, and our fathers, and to all the people of the land."
—Daniel 9:3–6

We want to blame everybody else—the company, the government, even other Christians. We point fingers everywhere, but when we have prayers that need to be answered, we must come to the place of confession.

When you have a loved one in the hospital clinging to life, a family member you want to witness to, a friend whose marriage is crumbling, you need God. If you don't confess the bitterness, envy, lust, or other sin in your heart, you are playing a game with God. The psalmist wrote, *"If I regard iniquity in my heart, the Lord will not hear me"* (Psalm 66:16).

Do you carry a burden for revival? Is it no more than a slight encumbrance, or is it a deep-seated burden for the moral problems in America? Are you willing to bring this burden to the Lord, fasting and humbly confessing that you have not always been the witness that you should be? Nehemiah's willingness to confess his sin was key to God's willingness to send revival.

Nehemiah's Prayer Was Based on the Promises of God

"Remember, I beseech thee, the word that thou commandedst thy servant Moses, saying, If ye transgress, I will scatter you abroad among the nations: But if ye turn unto me, and keep my commandments, and do them; though there were of you cast out unto the uttermost part of the heaven, yet will I gather them from thence, and will bring them unto the place that I have chosen to set my name there."—NEHEMIAH 1:8–9

What parent has not had his child remind him of previously made promises? "Remember when you said…" must be a phrase inherent in children, because they seem ready to wield this weapon as soon as they begin talking! Our children love to remind us of our promises.

As our Heavenly Father, God *wants* us to remind Him of His Word. He has given us *"exceeding great and precious promises"* (2 Peter 1:4), and He wants us to claim them in prayer. When we ignore God's promises, basing our prayers only on our own feelings or needs, we lose sight of God's desire to give to us.

While traveling with a group of pastors on a missions trip several years ago, we used a long layover in Thailand to take a walking tour of Bangkok. The streets bustled with peddlers calling out their wares trying to tempt tourists to buy, but one in particular caught my pastor-friend's attention. This peddler was selling Rolex watches for almost nothing.

I tried to explain to my friend that these were not genuine Rolex watches but cheap watches that illegally claimed the Rolex name. But persuaded by the persistent salesman, my friend bought a watch, feeling he had just made the purchase of a lifetime. He was terribly disappointed when, less than one day later, his watch stopped.

Unlike the "Rolex" salesman, God is able to deliver what He promises. When we discount or ignore God's promises, we demonstrate our lack of confidence in Him. We treat Him like we would treat a dishonest salesman. But when we, like Nehemiah, pray according to God's promises, we express our confidence in Him and in His Word.

After all, the ministry is not *our* idea; it is *God's* idea! He is the one who has placed you in your position of influence. He wants to bless you more than you want to be blessed. His promises are genuine, but He wants you to claim them through prayer.

Nehemiah's prayer instructs us in the order of God's work—pray first, and act second. Before Nehemiah lifted a trowel to build the walls, before he appealed for a single worker, he prayed. We have all made foolish and damaging decisions because we didn't pray before we acted.

If we will see revival, it will not begin with political reform, special evangelistic crusades, or even organized soulwinning canvassing. It will begin in the prayer closets of leaders who desire to make a difference.

When you are tempted to undertake God's work before you've prayed, remember Nehemiah on his knees before God, and remember the mighty work God wrought through his supplication.

CHAPTER FIVE

Revival Is Possible through Synergy

The 1988 centennial celebration in the small town of Bruno, Nebraska, was an incredible display of the power of synergy. Seven years earlier, Herman Ostry had purchased a farm, including a barn, half a mile out of town. In 1988 when spring flooding covered the barn floor with twenty-nine inches of water, Herman decided it was time to move the barn to higher ground.

The $1,500 estimate from professional movers was too steep, so Herman's son, Mike, devised another plan. He estimated that the barn weighed roughly 17,000 pounds. If 340 people carried fifty pounds each, they could simply carry the barn to its new location!

Mike built a grid of steel tubing around the barn and attached handles for the carriers. On July 30, over four thousand people from eleven different states watched as

344 people carried the barn about 120 feet. Minutes later, the barn was sitting on its new foundation.

What one person could never have accomplished alone, 344 people were able to do together. As someone once said, "teamwork makes the dream work."

The principle of synergy is that the combined efforts of two or more can produce more than each could produce individually. The Bible explains it this way: "*Two are better than one; because they have a good reward for their labour*" (Ecclesiastes 4:9).

When Jesus commissioned his disciples to preach, He sent them out in groups of two (Mark 6:7). He also promised special power in corporate prayer: "*For where two or three are gathered together in my name, there am I in the midst of them*" (Matthew 18:20).

During our church's first building program, we saw firsthand the power of corporate prayer. From the beginning of this project, we encountered a discouraging stream of opposition. Everything, from plans to budgets, seemed to take longer than we had anticipated. When we finally broke ground, we were thrilled!

To create a solid foundation in our desert soil, the construction crew had to first open a sixteen-foot hole and then fill it back in with heavy compactors. Between the times this hole was opened and filled, our area experienced record rainfall. Instead of our eight-inch yearly average rainfall, it seemed we were getting several inches every day! This continued for days and days, further postponing our building progress.

When we finally got the concrete poured and began framing, we encountered another obstacle—dispute between the foreman and the construction company. The foreman angrily left, taking our approved set of drawings to another state. We had to call the Arizona state police to retrieve our drawings!

Soon after the drawings were returned, our general contractor went bankrupt. Now we had plans but no builder. To make matters worse, the bank called and explained that because our loan approval had been contingent on our using that general contractor, they could no longer finance us.

One afternoon, a salesman from a pew company left a small sample pew for me to show our congregation as a money-raising visual. That Sunday night I explained to our church family that I would place the pew and a clipboard in the middle of the new building. I asked our people to come when they could throughout the week and kneel at that pew and pray for the building program. I also suggested that they write their name and the time they prayed on the clipboard.

I still have the papers our people signed. Many of our men left early for work, and I often saw them praying at four or five in the morning, some as early as one or two. There are many tear stains on those papers. This season of prayer was the turning point for our building program.

Within two weeks, a man from our community approached me about the building. His son was a sub-contractor and had told him about our lost financing. He loaned us $200,000 to keep the building moving until we could get our financing reapproved. We began contracting the building ourselves, and the work continued. When the bank financing finally did come through, we repaid this man with interest.

Today, this completed building stands as a testimony to the power of synergic prayer.

Leaders who attempt ministry alone are shorting themselves and the work of God. Synergy is essential to success.

To encourage others to join the team, a leader must first have a clear purpose. Nehemiah's purpose statement can be found in Nehemiah 2:10, *"…to seek the welfare of the children of Israel."*

Every city in this world needs men and women like Nehemiah who will come to seek their spiritual welfare through prayer, soulwinning, church planting—working for revival. Social reformers may provide temporary aid, but only God's truths can meet the deepest needs people face. Only the Gospel can make an eternal difference by promising all who believe a future home in Heaven.

Nehemiah's driving passion was the spiritual welfare of his people. A purpose of this magnitude could not be accomplished through simply dreaming, writing, or even delegating; this required his own personal involvement.

When God miraculously touched King Artaxerxes' heart, not only to allow Nehemiah's return to Jerusalem to rebuild the wall but also to provide him with all the resources he would need, Nehemiah was quick to step in.

This task, however, was far too great for one man alone; it required teamwork. Nehemiah's passion for this great work moved him to share his burden with others: *"Then said I unto them, Ye see the distress that we are in, how Jerusalem lieth waste, and the gates thereof are burned with fire: come, and let us build up the wall of Jerusalem, that we be no more a reproach"* (Nehemiah 2:17).

After sharing his burden, Nehemiah explained the opportunity the Lord had created for immediate action: *"Then I told them of the hand of my God which was good upon me; as also the king's words that he had spoken unto me. And they said, Let us rise up and build. So they strengthened their hands for this good work"* (Nehemiah 2:18).

A sure sign that someone believes in a cause is the energy he puts forth to recruit others' involvement. For example, have you ever seen the zeal with which ladies alert their family and friends to store specials? A person who is convinced of his cause is a thorn in the side of anyone who would remain uninvolved. This zealot is persuasive and, like a determined salesman, tries every means possible to enlist the support of others.

When Nehemiah shared his purpose, the people rallied behind him. *"And they said, Let us rise up and build. So they strengthened their hands for this good work"* (Nehemiah 2:18).

In many desperate situations, the greatest need is for a leader to exemplify causative leadership and state a clear purpose so that others will share his vision.

We find a great example of this truth in the hopeless war Judah faced against Assyria after Assyria had already conquered the northern kingdom of Israel. While God was, as always, able to work on behalf of His people, their fear threatened to turn them to other gods, thus forsaking their only hope for deliverance.

King Hezekiah was a leader who made a difference by challenging the people to share his vision of hope in God.

"Be strong and courageous, be not afraid nor dismayed for the king of Assyria, nor for all the multitude that is with him: for there be more with us than with him: With him is an arm of flesh; but with us is the LORD our God to help us, and to fight our battles. And the people rested themselves upon the words of Hezekiah king of Judah."—2 CHRONICLES 32:7–8

God miraculously delivered Judah from this battle, and He used one leader's call for synergy to give the people the faith they needed in God.

How clearly is your call for synergy sounding out? Who are you recruiting for God's work?

There is too much work before us for anyone to host a martyr complex and attempt to go it alone. Leaders who make a difference are men and women who involve others in effective teamwork. Nehemiah's leadership is an example of the power of synergy.

CHAPTER SIX

Revival Is Continued through Stamina

God's work can only be accomplished in God's strength because God's work never goes without opposition. Nehemiah's persistent focus was so strong that, in spite of many distractions, the wall was finished in fifty-two days. (That number makes me jealous every time I read it. Obviously, Nehemiah didn't have building inspectors, zoning regulations, local ordinances, or the countless codes we have today!)

The tests of stamina that Nehemiah faced, are the same tests we face today. Ours come with different names and faces, but our response must equal Nehemiah's if God is to be glorified.

Let's examine these tests and learn how we can sustain stamina through difficulties.

Persistent through Ridicule

"But when Sanballat the Horonite, and Tobiah the servant, the Ammonite, and Geshem the Arabian, heard it, they laughed us to scorn, and despised us, and said, What is this thing that ye do? will ye rebel against the king?"
—NEHEMIAH 2:19

No sooner had Nehemiah taken the first steps of preparation for this great work than the enemies of God's people began their mocking chants of ridicule.

The truth is, every noble work at first seems impossible; we don't need our enemies to tell us that! If the work is great enough to make an eternal difference, it is too great for our own resources.

Look at the Great Commission Christ gave the church: *"And he said unto them, Go ye into all the world, and preach the gospel to every creature"* (Mark 16:15). There are close to SEVEN billion people in the world, and we have been commanded to bring the Gospel to every one of them! That task is impossible with men, *"but with God all things are possible"* (Matthew 19:26).

Don't allow your critics' ridicule to sway your focus or your faith. The best way to deal with criticism is to, like Nehemiah, simply accomplish the task God has set before you.

Had Nehemiah shifted his energy from wall building to self defense, his attackers would have been successful—even if he had proven their insults to be wrong—because he would no longer be building the wall. Instead, Nehemiah wisely refused to become entangled in a war of words.

Refusing to entertain dialog with those who intended to destroy his work, Nehemiah gave a terse reply: *"Then answered I them, and said unto them, The God of heaven, he will prosper us; therefore we his servants will arise and build: but ye have no portion, nor right, nor memorial, in Jerusalem"* (Nehemiah 2:20).

Critics will try to involve you in psychological warfare, but you must refuse to lose your focus. I've made a vow to God that I will not let a critic set the agenda for my life. Many years ago, I gave my life to the Lord and to His work. How then can I allow an enemy of Christ to sidetrack me from this purpose?

God's servants are no stranger to the attacks of ridicule, disloyalty, or betrayal. Second Timothy 3:12 promises, *"Yea, and all that will live godly in Christ Jesus shall suffer persecution."* In other words, if you are serving God, you will face persecution. Sometimes your worst critics will even be blood relatives.

Our Baptist heritage is rich with leaders who made a difference through remaining faithful in persecution. I've had the privilege of visiting their grave sites in both Europe and America. The sacrifice of men like John Bunyan, who spent twelve years in prison for his faith, truly amazes and challenges me.

How is it that we are proud of the heritage of these who gave their very lives for Christ, but when someone says something to offend us, we want to quit? We need the stamina that comes from a realistic expectation of our enemy and an unshakable understanding of our purpose.

God's promises to the persecuted give us strength to remain faithful through ridicule:

"Blessed are ye, when men shall revile you, and persecute you, and shall say all manner of evil against you falsely, for my sake. Rejoice, and be exceeding glad: for great is your reward in heaven: for so persecuted they the prophets which were before you."—MATTHEW 5:11–12

"Beloved, think it not strange concerning the fiery trial which is to try you, as though some strange thing happened unto you: But rejoice, inasmuch as ye are partakers of Christ's sufferings; that, when his glory shall be revealed, ye may be glad also with exceeding joy. If ye be reproached for the name of Christ, happy are ye; for the spirit of glory and of God resteth upon you: on their part he is evil spoken of, but on your part he is glorified."—1 PETER 4:12–14

Rather than be destroyed by ridicule, we must come to the realization that ridicule is often confirmation that we are engaged in a great work—a work that requires God's almighty power.

Don't let ridicule discourage you. Stay in the work.

Persistent through Discouragement

"And Judah said, The strength of the bearers of burdens is decayed, and there is much rubbish; so that we are not able to build the wall."—Nehemiah 4:10

Ridicule was only the beginning of Nehemiah's difficulties! His building crew became so discouraged that all they could see was their waning strength and the piles of rubbish. (Incidentally, you must beware when all you can see is the negative aspects of your ministry work. When all you can think about is the rubbish, you are too distracted to build.)

In addition to the monumental task of wall building that lay before them, the people were fearful of the impending attack from their enemies.

Nehemiah did not allow the discouragement of others to cloud his vision or extinguish his determination. He developed a plan to alleviate the people's fears concerning the enemy, and he reminded the people of God's greatness and the worth of their cause (Nehemiah 4:13–14).

Perhaps you know through personal experience how tiring it is to lead discouraged people. Don't give up. Perhaps you have been battling discouraging circumstances for a long time. Keep on.

You never know how close you are to enjoying the fruit of your labor. Paul encouraged the Galatian believers: *"And let us not be weary in well doing: for in due season we shall reap, if we faint not"* (Galatians 6:9).

None of us have the physical, emotional, or spiritual resources to persevere through the most intense discouragement, but God does! And He has promised to renew our strength as we wait on Him: *"But they that wait upon the LORD shall renew their strength; they shall mount up with wings as eagles; they shall run, and not be weary; and they shall walk, and not faint"* (Isaiah 40:31).

Captain Timothy Stackpole, a New York firefighter, was severely burned in a 1998 fire. After months of rehabilitation, he insisted on returning to active duty in the late summer of 2001.

Many tried to encourage Timothy to take a desk job rather than again place himself in the front line of danger, but Timothy refused. "I have to rescue people. It's my duty—it's my calling," he insisted.

On September 11, 2001, Timothy was driving home from work when he heard the call for rescue workers to the World Trade Center. He turned around and hurried to the twin towers. Immediately he organized a group of rescuers and rushed into the burning building to help people to safety. Minutes later the tower he was in collapsed, and he gave his life.

Is your commitment to your calling that strong? If God has called you to a position of leadership, don't give up when the discouraging times come. Be a leader who makes a difference, even when you are tempted to quit.

Persistent through Temptation to Compromise

"Now it came to pass, when Sanballat, and Tobiah, and Geshem the Arabian, and the rest of our enemies, heard that I had builded the wall, and that there was no breach left therein; (though at that time I had not set up the doors upon the gates;) That Sanballat and Geshem sent unto me, saying, Come, let us meet together in some one of the villages in the plain of Ono. But they thought to do me mischief."
—Nehemiah 6:1–2

When Nehemiah's enemies saw they could not succeed in a frontal attack, they shifted their tactics. Now, instead of coming with spears and bows, they called for an ecumenical meeting—a meeting of compromise.

Nehemiah, however, was not naïve. He knew better than to believe that the same men who days earlier were attacking his life's work were really sincere in wanting to aid him in friendship. Five times these enemies called him to this meeting, and five times he refused to entertain even a simple conversation.

Nehemiah's reply reveals his dedication: *"And I sent messengers unto them, saying, I am doing a great work, so that I cannot come down: why should the work cease, whilst I leave it, and come down to you?"* (Nehemiah 6:1–3).

We, too, are involved in a great work—taking the Gospel to every corner of the globe. We have no time to give to lesser pursuits. When the temptation to compromise comes, keep your eyes on the greatness of your work for Christ.

Satan will tempt you to compromise your doctrine and your convictions through foolish alliances with those who defame the name of Christ. To avoid these traps, you must, like Nehemiah, become a separated leader with discernment.

In Philippians 1:9–10, Paul prayed this prayer for the Philippian church: *"that your love may abound yet more and more in knowledge and in all judgment; That ye may approve things that are excellent; that ye may be sincere and without offence till the day of Christ"* (Philippians 1:9–10). Gaining discernment is one way your love for God will grow and strengthen; you must avoid those who would draw you away from the Lord or His truth.

Refuse to build friendships with or study after those who deny the authority of God's Word and teach principles contrary to God's. Beware of those who encourage you to conform your convictions to the world's standards rather than determine your convictions from God's standards.

The work of God requires stamina. Nehemiah sustained his stamina even through staggering difficulties. He persisted through both ridicule and discouragement, and he remained faithful when tempted to compromise.

This tenacity is required of leaders who will make a difference. Will you crumble under the pressures, or will you face the trials with God's strength?

Many today question the possibility of revival. These naysayers see only the decaying moral condition of society and the disappointing lukewarm condition of churches. Revival, however, is not dependent on or the result of a flourishing spiritual condition. Some of the greatest revivals in Scripture came during the darkest times.

Let us not look at the rubbish, but at Christ, the Rock, who can rebuild our country through revival. Let us be leaders God can use to bring revival.

Nehemiah was not a man to sit idly by when there was tremendous need. Neither was he a man to attempt meeting such need in his own strength. God used Nehemiah to bring revival because Nehemiah began with supplication for God's forgiveness and power.

The task of rebuilding the walls could never have been completed by one man alone; it needed a leader who understood the power of synergy. Nehemiah's willingness to be personally involved in the work, as well as his ability to convey the need to others, resulted in a task force that completed this enormous building project in a mere fifty-two days—to the glory of God.

Like any godly leader, Nehemiah did not go unchallenged. Yet, he sustained his stamina in the face of every opposition.

Nehemiah's life proves that revival is possible, even when it appears the most unlikely. God sends revival through leaders willing to make a difference.

PART THREE

Joseph

A LEADER WHO FINISHED WELL

If there was ever a man who could have justified quitting, it was Joseph. It seemed that with every choice Joseph made to honor God, his difficulties increased. Yet, in the last chapter of Genesis, Joseph finishes his race with a sweet spirit.

There is no guarantee that every Christian leader will finish his spiritual race strong. In fact, many don't. Both Scripture and history record accounts of many leaders who possessed every advantage to win their races with flying colors but relented to difficulty before experiencing victory.

I believe we would all like to say with Paul, "*I have fought a good fight, I have finished my course, I have kept the faith*" (2 Timothy 4:7).

Finishing the race doesn't happen by accident. Let's examine what brought Joseph to the finish line and how we, too, can finish with joy.

CHAPTER SEVEN

Finishing Well Begins with Faith

A Christian's race is not just difficult—it is impossible. Thus faith is essential to the Christian life, for *"without faith it is impossible to please [God]"* (Hebrews 11:6).

Faith can simply be defined as "trusting God." Only God knows where our life's course will lead. Only God knows the difficulties we will encounter and the battles we will face. And only God has the resources to strengthen us through these difficulties, empowering us to finish victoriously.

Joseph recognized that God alone could get him across the finish line, and he placed his faith in God's promises.

Before the Bible was completely recorded by man, God often revealed His will through dreams. He gave Joseph two prophetic dreams revealing that he would one day be in a position of leadership over his eleven brothers.

Joseph, the second youngest brother, had no idea of how God would fulfill this dream or of the difficulties he would face before it became reality, but he still believed it. In fact, he believed it so fully that he shared it with his family.

It's one thing to hear God's truth, but it's another thing entirely to share your beliefs with others. Many times others (even your own family members) don't understand or appreciate your faith in God. In Joseph's case, sharing this revelation from God caused his brothers to despise him (Genesis 37:8).

What truth has God given you? Today God reveals His truth through His written Word. Peter, who experienced God's Word in both spoken and written forms, described the written Word as *"a more sure word of prophecy"* (2 Peter 1:19).

Leaders who finish well have the faith to trust God's Word—its promises and its commands. They are willing to step out in faith, in obedience to God's revealed will for their lives, even if they cannot see where that step will take them.

As Corrie Ten Boom aptly pointed out, we should "never be afraid to trust an unknown future to a known God." Our faith must be centered on God Himself.

When my family and I first came to Lancaster Baptist Church, we had no solid financial foundation. We had just spent all of our savings on moving and in fixing the building and the property of our new church.

With no money in the bank and no salary from the church, we based our assurance that all would be well on God's promises. Our faith was not misplaced, for we never missed a meal or saw our needs unmet.

Twenty-three years later, I'm so thankful we came to Lancaster even before we knew what God was going to do here. When I see how God has blessed this ministry, it motivates me to take further steps of faith.

What in your life requires faith? When God gives a leader a vision of His plan for his life or ministry, it's far greater than what can be accomplished in human strength. Refuse to question God's ability; instead trust God's plan.

Faith is not an emotion fueled by success stories or emotionally charged sermons. Faith is a simple choice to trust God.

Romans 10:17 describes how we gain faith: *"So then faith cometh by hearing, and hearing by the word of God."* The Bible is integral to building faith. A leader who spends no time hearing the Word of God is a leader of weak faith.

God's Word must be given the preeminence in our own lives, and then in our ministry. Too many leaders starve their faith with inadequate spiritual diets. Having spent little time in God's Word, they wonder why they are spiritually emaciated!

Friend, there is no substitute for purposeful time daily spent in God's Word. How can you cling to promises you do not know? How can you follow directions you have not heard? How can you lead where you have not been?

Those we look to as great spiritual leaders have been men and women who loved God's Word. Hudson Taylor, a fifty-one-year missionary to China and founder of the China Inland Mission, often rose at 5:00 AM to spend two hours with the Lord before starting his work. Near the end of his life, he wrote, "The sun has never risen in China without finding me on my knees." No wonder Taylor had the faith that saw thousands of missionaries open inland China with the Gospel!

George Müller, founder of orphanages in England said that for every page of a Bible commentary, he read ten pages of Scripture. This godly man saturated his soul with the Bible, reading it through over one hundred times. No wonder Müller had the faith to build five large orphanages and care for 10,024 orphans—all with no salary!

Evangelist D.L. Moody was also known as a diligent student of the Bible. He rose early every morning (often at 4:00) to spend time in God's Word. He said, "If I am going to get in any study, I have got to get up before the other folks get up." No wonder Moody had the faith to shake two continents for Christ!

Job had a clear perspective of our dependence on God's Word when he wrote, *"I have esteemed the words of his mouth more than my necessary food"* (Job 23:12). If you are struggling to maintain consistent Bible reading, make a commitment that will help you with your priorities— determine that you will not eat until you have spent time in God's Word that day.

Leaders of great faith are men and women who read, study, and love God's Word. D.L. Moody wrote, "I never saw a useful Christian who was not a student of the Bible."

Faith is essential to God's power for God has *"chosen the weak things of the world to confound the things which are mighty"* (1 Corinthians 1:27). When we trust God's revealed plan, even when it is far beyond our power to orchestrate, God gets the glory.

Joseph was given a vision far greater than he could ever manipulate into reality. Only God could accomplish this in Joseph's life, and Joseph trusted that God would.

When Joseph first trusted God's plan, he had no idea how it would come to pass. But fast forward a few years in Joseph's life, and the situation looked more bleak than ever. His brothers sold him into slavery. Later, in Egypt he was promoted to leadership, only to be incarcerated in a dungeon for a crime he did not commit. Nearly thirteen years had passed since he first received the vision. Did he still trust God's plan? Was his faith still strong?

We find the answer in a statement he made to Pharaoh while interpreting Pharaoh's dream: *"And for that the dream was doubled unto Pharaoh twice; it is because the thing is established by God, and God will shortly bring it to pass"* (Genesis 41:32). Joseph, too, had been given a "doubled dream," and in faith he held onto the belief that God indeed intended to fulfill this vision.

Joseph's faith was rewarded with God's supernatural power working on his behalf.

Scripture specifically describes two men as *"full of faith"*—Stephen (Acts 6:5, 8) and Barnabas (Acts 11:24). Both of these men were also "full of the Holy Ghost."

To be leaders who make a difference, we need the Holy Spirit's power. This power is not only vital to our ministries, but it is given in proportion to our faith and submission to Him.

Joseph's spectacular ending was rooted in a solid beginning—faith in God. If we will finish well, we must start with faith. Faith is an essential. It is what legs are to a runner, what wheels are to a bicycle, what an engine is to a vehicle. A strong finish is not possible without faith.

Does God's plan for your life seem utterly impossible? I hope so! Leaders who make a difference must be leaders of faith—*"Have faith in God"* (Mark 11:22).

CHAPTER EIGHT

Finishing Well Is Accomplished through Faithfulness

As exciting as the prospects of faith are, it is often a long time before we see the results of faith. This was certainly the case in Joseph's life. Approximately thirteen years passed between the dreams God gave him and God's fulfillment of those dreams.

In the meantime, Joseph faced one seemingly insurmountable obstacle after another. He had many opportunities to drop out of the race, yet he expressed his faith in God through his faithfulness to God.

Leaders who neglect their faithfulness to God demonstrate their lack of faith in God. Those who don't finish their race have chosen to remove themselves from God's protection and power.

Anyone can be faithful when the sun is shining and life feels grand, but it is faithfulness through the dark nights and lonely valleys that proves genuine faith.

A faith that cannot be tested cannot be trusted, so God often tests our faith. If the test reveals continued faithfulness to God, our faith brings glory to God and honors Him in the eyes of all who observe the test.

The circumstances God allowed in Joseph's life are staggering. Most of us would struggle with faithfulness if any one of these situations occurred, but Joseph remained true through all of them.

When He Was Betrayed by His Brothers

"And his brethren envied him...And Judah said unto his brethren, What profit is it if we slay our brother, and conceal his blood? Come, and let us sell him to the Ishmeelites, and let not our hand be upon him; for he is our brother and our flesh. And his brethren were content."—GENESIS 37:11, 26–27

This betrayal began with a sinister envy. Joseph's brothers envied the favoritism their father displayed for Joseph. They also envied the special revelation he received from God.

Envy is often the root of spiteful words and actions. Those who are carnal are simply too self-centered to be happy when someone else is blessed.

Joseph's brothers became so bitter toward Joseph that they wanted to get rid of him once and for all. When Joseph's father sent him to take supplies to his brothers who were out grazing flocks, his brothers made plans to kill him: *"Come now therefore, and let us slay him, and cast him into some pit, and we will say, Some evil beast hath devoured him: and we shall see what will become of his dreams"* (Genesis 37:20).

I have noticed that whenever a leader dares to utter his God-given dreams (from raising a godly family to building a church to establishing a Christ-honoring business), there are always those who say, "Oh, yeah? We'll see what will become of that dream." When you have the faith to believe God's plan and share it with others, expect opposition.

Joseph's opposition came in the form of his own brothers selling him into slavery. Scripture even records that after they made the decision to sell him, they *"were content"* (Genesis 37:27).

Have you ever felt that others would be happy if you failed? Perhaps you have co-workers who would be glad to get one of the "born-again Christians" out of the office. Perhaps your family opposes you and prophesies that your consecration toward God will bring destruction into your life.

When envious and hateful opposition comes your way, remember Joseph. He was a good man, a man of faith, but for his faith, he was despised by his own family.

If you look for opportunities to quit, there will be plenty of them. Every leader encounters many opportunities to drop out of the race, but even in the face of betrayal, Joseph remained faithful.

Someone defined integrity as "keeping my commitment even if the circumstances when I made the commitment have changed." Joseph was a man of integrity who remained true to his commitment to his God.

I've seen men and women keep their marriage commitments even when cancer or other severe health difficulties have changed their circumstances. I've seen Christian businessmen keep their commitments to customers and employees even when unforeseen price increases changed the circumstances. I've seen mothers and fathers keep their promises to their children even when scheduling conflicts changed the circumstances.

This sort of integrity is the mark of a spiritually mature leader. When circumstances change in your life, retain your integrity. Don't curse God, but praise Him.

The day that Joseph's brothers betrayed him changed his life forever. But while his circumstances changed, his faithfulness remained steadfast.

When He Was Tempted by His Boss's Wife

"And it came to pass after these things, that his master's wife cast her eyes upon Joseph; and she said, Lie with me. But he

refused, and said unto his master's wife, Behold, my master wotteth not what is with me in the house, and he hath committed all that he hath to my hand; There is none greater in this house than I; neither hath he kept back any thing from me but thee, because thou art his wife: how then can I do this great wickedness, and sin against God?"—GENESIS 39:7–9

Sometimes a Christian's faithfulness is tested through trials, and sometimes it is tested through temptations. The devil doesn't care which method wipes you out; he just wants to be sure he gets the job done. After Joseph endured the deep wound of betrayal, another hardship came—temptation.

After being brought to Egypt, Joseph quickly rose to a position of authority in his master's house because of his integrity. Potiphar, his master and a high-ranking officer in the Egyptian army, gave Joseph control over everything he owned—except his wife.

Potiphar's lewd and immoral wife set her eyes on Joseph. When she tried to seduce him, he fled from her pursuits, demonstrating his faith in God through faithfulness to God.

What a tremendous example Joseph is to us! When this wicked woman tried to entice him, he retained his integrity. He could have made excuses that would have satisfied the flesh, but he recognized that this sin would be against God.

Joseph was a great leader because he lived with the fear of God. He was aware of God's presence even in

Egypt, and he remained faithful to God's commands even when no one else was watching.

Although our sin does deeply wound others, it is not primarily others we hurt when we cave in to temptation. Sin is *always* against God.

After David's sin with Bathsheba he recognized this truth. In his psalm of repentance he wrote, *"Against thee, thee only, have I sinned, and done this evil in thy sight: that thou mightest be justified when thou speakest, and be clear when thou judgest"* (Psalm 51:4). When we sin, we shame the name of our Lord. This knowledge should motivate us to hate sin.

Notice that Satan sent this moral temptation to Joseph while he was still reeling from the blow of betrayal. Satan never plays fair. He will accost you with temptation when you are most vulnerable.

Joseph's purity is a testimony to each of us that faithfulness to God is possible, even under intense temptation.

When He Was Falsely Accused

"And Joseph's master took him, and put him into the prison, a place where the king's prisoners were bound: and he was there in the prison."—GENESIS 39:20

Joseph's faithfulness during temptation was immediately rewarded with false accusation and imprisonment. After failing to seduce Joseph, Potiphar's wife framed Joseph and accused him of attempted rape! Because of this false accusation, Joseph was thrown into prison.

If there was ever a low point in Joseph's life, this was it. When he was betrayed, he remained faithful; when he was tempted, he remained faithful; and even when he was falsely accused, he remained faithful. But for all his faithfulness, he continued to sink into progressively worse circumstances—finally prison.

If Joseph had been like many men, he would have eventually succumbed to bitterness. He could have said, "I tried it God's way, and this is all I get? Forget it!" But not Joseph—he *continued* to express faith through his faithfulness to God.

Even through these dark days, God's mercy sustained Joseph. Even when circumstances indicated otherwise, God was near His servant during the testing.

Four times Scripture specifically points to God's presence in Joseph's life. *"But the LORD was with Joseph, and shewed him mercy, and gave him favour in the sight of the keeper of the prison"* (Genesis 39:21).

I don't know what the keeper of the prison did to show favor to Joseph. Perhaps he brought him hamburgers after hours or sneaked him a Snickers bar every so often. Whatever the method, God used this man to give Joseph tokens of God's love for him.

God's continual presence is the guaranteed provision of every child of God. Every leader will be tested. Whatever the test, however dark the valley, remember that the God who was with Joseph will *"never leave thee nor forsake thee"* (Hebrews 13:5).

Even when clouds conceal the path ahead and when your way twists through valleys of loss, look for God's tokens of love for you. He has not forgotten you; His mercy will sustain you; and He will send a "keeper of the prison" to remind you of His care.

We see the overview of Joseph's life—we can read the whole story in a few chapters. But Joseph lived it one day at a time. The years he spent in prison dragged out with loneliness and anguish. But even in his affliction, he was faithful.

Joseph's life at this point appears to be a dismal failure. God, however, does not require success; He requires faithfulness: *"Moreover it is required in stewards, that a man be found faithful"* (1 Corinthians 4:2).

Joseph's faithfulness was not only tested, it was rewarded! By the end of his life, he was ruling the entire land of Egypt, and his brothers were eating out of his hand, just as in his dream.

Why was he blessed? Through his faithfulness to God, he expressed his faith in God, fulfilling God's dream for him. In times of plenty he was faithful, and in times of sorrow he was faithful. God saw and blessed his faithfulness.

Never listen to Satan when he suggests that God has forgotten or ignored your faithfulness to Him. God sees when your finances are tight, but you faithfully tithe. He sees when your own heart is breaking, but you faithfully minister to others. He sees when your health fails, but you faithfully find ways to serve Him. He sees when, even through uncertainty and disappointment, you faithfully put one foot in front of the other and continue on for Him.

Paul knew what it was to press on through difficulty. He wrote, *"We are troubled on every side, yet not distressed; we are perplexed, but not in despair; Persecuted, but not forsaken; cast down, but not destroyed"* (2 Corinthians 4:8–9).

Refuse to quit during the tough times. These are the greatest opportunities we have to express our faith in Christ through our faithfulness to Him. Anyone can be faithful when the road is smooth, but only those who trust in God's unwavering goodness will persevere with faithfulness on the rocky climbs.

God sees your faithfulness, and He will reward you for it. *"For God is not unrighteous to forget your work and labour of love, which ye have shewed toward his name, in that ye have ministered to the saints, and do minister"* (Hebrews 6:10).

Just keep trusting your Lord. *"And let us not be weary in well doing: for in due season we shall reap, if we faint not"* (Galatians 6:9).

Joseph's faithfulness to God shines like a beacon giving direction when circumstances attempt to overwhelm us. Whatever comes your way, remain faithful to your God.

CHAPTER NINE

Finishing Well Requires Forgiveness

According to Joseph's original dream, his brothers came to him for help. At this point, both Egypt and Canaan were in the midst of a severe famine, but because of God's providential hand on Joseph, Egypt had food in storage.

As overseer of the food distribution, Joseph saw his brothers when they came for food. Because Joseph had adapted to the Egyptian culture in his appearance and manner, his brothers did not recognize him.

Surely this was his chance to repay his brothers for the grief they had caused him! These were the men who had at one point intended to kill him but instead opted for the financial gain of selling him into slavery. These were the callous men responsible for his hardships—separation from his father, slavery, and unjust imprisonment. He could withhold food or at least make them grovel for it. But great leaders forgive, and Joseph was a great leader.

There's not a CEO of a company who hasn't had someone mistreat him. There's not a parent who hasn't had a broken heart over a child. There's not a police officer who hasn't been falsely accused of abusing his authority.

Every leader is given plenty of opportunities to become bitter, but wallowing in resentment and bitterness only hurts oneself. I've seen mothers destroy their families through bitterness toward the pastor or another member of the church. I've seen families ripped apart by bitterness over an offence that no one even remembers any more. Truly, bitterness hurts the vessel in which it is stored more than the vessel on which it is poured.

One of the clearest signs of Joseph's greatness was his ability to endure without resentment. Joseph's forgiveness was the overflow of a heart of love. He had endured hardness without becoming hard himself. His tender heart was evidenced by his tears when he saw his brothers.

Imagine the shock his brothers experienced when Joseph revealed his identity with the simple words *"I am Joseph"* (Genesis 45:3). Their consciences were so troubled that they *"could not answer him."*

Here they stood before their brother—the ruler of Egypt—whom they had sold into slavery. What would he do to them? How would he punish them?

But Joseph's response was one of grace. *"And he said, I am Joseph your brother, whom ye sold into Egypt. Now therefore be not grieved, nor angry with yourselves, that ye sold me hither: for God did send me before you to preserve life"* (Genesis 45:4–5).

In many ways, Joseph is a picture of Christ. Both were:

- loved by their father
- rejected by their brothers
- victorious over temptation
- sold for the equivalent of one day's wage
- taken into custody because of a false witness
- persecuted for doing what was right

But one of the most touching similarities is their forgiveness. Joseph could have snuffed out his brothers by speaking a word, but he chose to forgive. Jesus could have wiped us off the planet, but He *laid down His life* to give us the mercy of forgiveness.

What is there, then, that we cannot forgive? Ephesians 4:32 admonishes, *"And be ye kind one to another, tenderhearted, forgiving one another, even as God for Christ's sake hath forgiven you."*

Forgiveness is a choice. We often have opportunity to injure those who have injured us, but when we choose to forgive, we progress light years ahead in our spiritual growth.

How could Joseph make this choice? So many Christians seem to lose their spiritual discernment because they can't forgive the people who have wronged them. What was Joseph's secret?

Joseph focused on the Lord rather than on his pain. He did not reach this stance of forgiveness by psychological methods of tricking his mind to believe the situation was different from what it was. In fact, he candidly told his brothers, *"But as for you, ye thought evil against me."* But then he ended the statement, *"but God meant it unto good, to bring to pass, as it is this day, to save much people alive"* (Genesis 50:20).

Here was a man who understood the sovereign plan of God. He saw from a heavenly perspective. A spiritual leader is always looking for God's hand in a problem. He knows he can't control the problem, but he searches for God's working through the problem.

Have you come to the place in your life where, when offences come, you can step back and say, "Lord, I don't understand all of this, but I trust You, and I will wait to see Your reasons"?

Some optimistic people can, in Pollyanna fashion, find ways to capitalize on the good in an otherwise bad situation. But only God can take a situation that has nothing but bad and sovereignly turn it into something wonderful and beneficial.

There was nothing good about Joseph's brothers selling him into slavery. Without God's supernatural ordering of hearts and events, Joseph would have simply rotted in an Egyptian dungeon. But Joseph knew better than to look at his life from a human perspective. It could only be explained by God's amazing grace.

When we focus on the offences we suffer from others, constantly reliving the details of the pain they have inflicted, we miss the wonderful view from the summit of faith.

You can keep score of the offences that come your way, storing them in a mental gunny sack, but if you do, you must carry this load of unforgiveness everywhere you go. A better choice is to dump them all out at Jesus' feet and ask for His help to forgive.

When we release our offences, we are able to focus on God's sovereignty that works all things *"together for good to them that love God, to them who are the called according to his purpose"* (Romans 8:28).

Joseph not only chose to forgive his brothers, but he put feet to his forgiveness by meeting his brothers' tangible needs. He promised them, *"I will nourish you, and your little ones. And he comforted them, and spake kindly unto them"* (Genesis 50:21).

I once heard a story of two brothers who were rice farmers in China. Daily, they had to haul enormous amounts of water to flood their rice paddies.

To retain the water for their rice fields, the brothers built a dike around the fields. Their neighbor, a lost man, was also a rice farmer, and a lazy one at that. To save himself the work of hauling water, this neighbor began breaking down part of the dike separating his field from the brothers' field.

Trying to practice Christian love and forgiveness, the brothers simply repaired the dike and carried more water. But inside they were eaten up by bitterness towards their neighbor.

After several days of this trouble, they asked their pastor about it. "Why," they asked, "can't we seem to forgive our neighbor from the heart?" Their pastor explained the principle that Joseph practiced—finding a tangible way to meet the offender's needs.

The next morning, before the brothers began the backbreaking labor of hauling water for their own fields, they first flooded their neighbor's rice paddy. They later told their pastor that this act of sacrifice released their bitterness and gave them genuine love for their neighbor. Shortly after, as a result of this demonstration of Christ's love and forgiveness, their neighbor trusted Christ as his Saviour.

Is there someone you need to forgive? What could you do to serve the one who has hurt you?

Finishing well for God does not mean finishing perfectly—we are all a "work in progress." Finishing well does not mean finishing uninjured—we will all be wounded, sometimes even by those who are closest to us. Finishing well does not mean finishing with a bestowal of human accolades—we measure success differently than God does.

Finishing well does mean finishing. Don't drop out of the race. The endurance to stay in the race requires faith in God's Word, faithfulness to God's will, and forgiveness by focusing on God's character.

"Wherefore seeing we also are compassed about with so great a cloud of witnesses, let us lay aside every weight, and the sin which doth so easily beset us, and let us run with patience the race that is set before us, Looking unto Jesus the author and finisher of our faith; who for the joy that was set before him endured the cross, despising the shame, and is set down at the right hand of the throne of God."—Hebrews 12:1–2

To be a leader who makes a difference, you must finish the race.

Conclusion

The lives of these leaders are a testimony to us that godly leadership isn't about one's position on a flowchart or status in society. It's not about who you know or where you're from. *"For promotion cometh neither from the east, nor from the west, nor from the south. But God is the judge: he putteth down one, and setteth up another"* (Psalm 75:6–7).

Leadership is influence, and God has given all of us a measure of influence. Fathers, mothers, Sunday school teachers, bus workers, deacons, pastors, church leaders, missionaries, students, grandparents—everyone has been entrusted with an influence that is uniquely his. Leaders who make a difference are wise stewards of that influence.

In these pages, we examined three different leaders whom God used in incredible ways.

Many of the patterns in these men's lives were repeated. They each endured a period of waiting; they each faced strong, almost overwhelming opposition; they each endured intense temptation.

These similarities show us that as God is creating beautiful portraits of leadership, He uses similar techniques—sometimes bold strokes and dark shades—to develop each unique portrait into a balanced composition.

These men could not see how their pictures would turn out while the partially painted canvas still contained rough sketching. But each one submitted to the Artist's skillful hand, displaying some of the leadership God was creating even as the picture was taking shape.

You cannot know yet what picture God is painting in your life. But you can choose to trust His mastery and submit to the plan He has sketched.

We have examined nine specific traits God blesses in leaders. Surrender yourself to Him, and allow Him to develop these traits in your life.

The larger canvas of this world has never been in greater need of leaders who will make a difference. Use the resources God has given you to make a difference in your sphere of influence for God's glory.

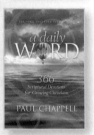

Visit us online

strivingtogether.com

dailyintheword.org

wcbc.edu

lancasterbaptist.org

paulchappell.com